The Real Estate Primer

The Golden Rules of Buying and Selling

by Geoffrey Gibson

Modern History Press

Library of Congress Cataloging-in-Publication Data

Gibson, Geoffrey (Geoffrey Hope), 1937-
  The real estate primer : the golden rules of buying and selling / by Geoffrey Gibson.
     page cm
  ISBN 978-1-61599-228-7 (pbk. : alk. paper) -- ISBN (invalid) 978-1-61599-229-4 (ebook)
  1. House buying. 2. House selling. 3. Real estate investment. 4. Residential real estate. I. Title.
  HD1379.G525 2014
  643'.12--dc23
                                              2014006545

Modern History Press, an imprint of L.H. Press
5145 Pontiac Trail
Ann Arbor, MI 48105

www.ModernHistoryPress.com
info@ModernHistoryPress.com

Tollfree (USA/CAN): 888-761-6268
FAX: 734-663-6861

Dedication

For my granddaughter Madeleine, whose arrival served to spur me on to get this book published. It is my sincere wish that one day she and others of her generation will be able to purchase a home.

Contents

Preface

As real estate agent and valuer for many years I've always found it a treat to deal with a client who was obviously well informed. It avoided the muddle and disappointment of not being able to conclude the purchase or sale. I am hopeful that my readers will realize how essential it is that both parties have faithfully done their basic research so they can confidently be part of a successful negotiation.

Why?

Having put in the groundwork, coaxing the two parties into the position where they have enough information and feel confident enough to negotiate is an achievement all on its own. To get them to where they can complete their deal is the reason I have written this guide.

Geoffrey Hope Gibson.

Chapter 1 – Buying a Home.

For most of us, buying a home is the biggest financial undertaking we will ever make, and it is important that we get it right. "The agents I deal with have been absolutely charming," you say. Exactly, the successful ones always are. This book is all about guiding you through the business of buying or selling a property. I have written this guide because after thirty years as a real estate agent and valuer on the Lower North Shore of Sydney, Australia I find the need for a decent primer even greater now than when I started all those years ago.

Perhaps it is the pace at which we live. We are bombarded with information from all directions and most of it is irrelevant to what we need. Our cell phones can tell us what is happening all over the world. We are pulled one way and then another as pundits tell us what is hot and what is not. We need to withdraw from all this information overload and set a clear goal of what we want to do and then concentrate on achieving it.

For some people, the idea of borrowing such an enormous amount of money and undertaking to pay it back is simply overwhelming. Others set out on the journey in the belief that they don't think they can have much influence on the outcome. Let me assure you, they can and they should. How many friends have you seen obsess over choosing a refrigerator or the new family car, the value of which will plummet as soon as they leave the showroom? I have often thought that people spend more time researching those purchases than they do on buying their home.

This booklet was written for conditions in Sydney, Australia, but the principles of getting out there and doing your basic research are the same wherever you are. Here the legal obligation is for the agent to operate on the vendor's behalf. However, they may be specifically employed to act as a buyer's agent. This basic understanding is very important, so check out how the legal obligations work in the market wherever you intend to buy or sell.

Enough preaching from me, as now it is time for reality and I would like you and your partner to contemplate the following.

> "I set out into the property market alone, therefore I must learn all I can about the transaction I am about to make, since nobody else can learn or make it for me. The money I make, save or lose in the transaction is my responsibility and no one else's. I understand that real estate agents and their sales staff normally act only for the vendor. They operate in a marketplace and are heavily influenced by their need to make constant sales to survive. Nor do they provide a free property finding and buying service, and should not be confused with a specifically appointed buyer's agent. Therefore, I must do my own research as my and their interests differ."

Our research is underway and we begin to collect our data. The first thing you should have is an improvised spreadsheet ruled with vertical columns, which will probably run over two pages. Use it to record the details of each property you inspect across the page: that is the address, a brief description, the agent and their phone number, the date it came on, whether it is a sale by auction or by private treaty (PT), when it was sold and the sale price. Treat the result of a sale by treaty or auction as being exactly the same. The most important item we are after is the sale price. For our purposes it is worth its weight in gold, and hearsay or approximations will not do.

Your spreadsheet might look something like this:

Address	Description	Auction or PT?	Agent	Result	Notes
215 Maple Leaf Drv, Lower Portland	1970's Painted **brick house** rend Span red tile, 4br,2 bath nice ord. worn kit. Air-con noisy. 3 car garage	Priv Trt Auc 7/4/2012	JPY ptners 7349 2534.	Sold $730, 000	Garden Uneven 3 levels. Old pool
47A Ocean Rd Boat Harbour.	2005 brick on concrete footings. We like it, great views, nice layout. Great kitchen huge open plan. 4 br 3 bath Boat storage 4 car garage	PT $745,000	Middleton Jones 0658 3317 Jack Moran 0942 1394		Nice heated Pool Sandstone flagging

Already, things are falling into place, and you are beginning to educate yourself in what properties are selling for and therefore honing your buying and selling skills. There are no short cuts, as it is essential to know the price of similar properties. You just have to get out into the marketplace and methodically go through the properties that are for sale, then do your inspections.

You cannot inspect too many properties. After all,

this is what effective agents have to do all day. I suggest you set a goal to inspect, say, forty or so. See as many as you can that are similar to the sort of home you would like to buy, and follow them through until you have recorded their sale price. A word about the time frame for this. Auctions and private treaty sales take some weeks to evolve, so you will have to follow them up and call the agent, ask at the local municipal council or subscribe to a service to get the sale price. Do it together with your partner and make a game of it, and along the way a nice lunch is a pleasant thing to do.

Think about it, if you skimp on your research, you are setting yourself up to be well and truly screwed. The aim is to train yourself to walk into a property and to be able to accurately assess its value.

You must compare like with like, so do not compare a clad or veneer home with a brick one, or a four bedroom home with two bathrooms with a three bedroom home with one bathroom. Do not compare a home with large level land with one on a small block, nor a home in a busy street with one in a quite leafy one.

Same goes for strata titled apartments, or those with other titles such as company or tenancy in common, but always like with like. Compare apartments in small buildings with those also in small buildings of similar age and location. Compare apartments in a large multi rise with those also in a large multi rise of a similar age and location.

There is no more important task, so stick with it, attend openings and auctions sales, and see how close you can get to predicting the result. When your predictions start to be accurate you are getting there. The reward is that when you see something that is really good buying, you will immediately recognize it.

Talk to and get to know the agents. You never know, they might just be the one who produces the perfect home for you. Already you are growing in confidence and provided you can find "the home," it will not be long before you are ready to buy.

Now, let us assume that after some weeks of research, and diving in and out of properties, an agent rings up with a message that might go something like this, "last night our agency listed a new home, which I think you will like, and I would like to show it to you."

It turns out to be exactly what you want, which brings us to the hurdle of price.

Realizing that as charming and helpful as they are, you and the real estate salespeople have different goals. Theirs is to produce a buyer who has approved finance and to negotiate the highest price they can, and for the sale to take place without any difficulties. Only when this has happened will they be paid their commission.

Your goal is to buy the property, aware of all its faults, for the lowest price you can.

Ah, the value of our research.

We find there is a big difference between what our research is telling us the property is worth, and the price the owner wants.

May we pause for a moment, for it is a free world out there and the owners are entitled to ask whatever price they fancy.

That is all very well, but it is also true that the real estate market finds its own level according to the economic reality of the time. When buyers are dominant it goes up, and the reverse is also true, so that when sellers take over it goes down. When they are in balance, the real estate market stays steady.

This property represents something of a dilemma: it has everything we want in a home, the kitchen is perfect, and the agent says they are expecting triplets and are selling to buy a larger home. However, according to our research it would be smarter to buy a cheaper, similar styled home in an adjoining suburb and have it painted, carpeted and to have a new kitchen installed. And our figures show we would be a mile in front.

Which turns out not to be a dilemma at all. What has happened is that our research is telling us that the owners of this home are too ambitious, and that they and their agent have put far too much money on it. Great, at least we have determined that it is they who are out of step with the market and not ourselves.

It is probably time for me to reveal to you of one of the most important truisms of the property market, which is this:

"The cost of <u>improvements</u> does not equal value."

I am indebted to the late Harry Thomas, who was the Chief Valuer of the Commonwealth Bank of Australia, for drilling this concept into his students, of which I was fortunate to be one.

Please remember it, as it is often the reason why major developers and property owners unexpectedly go broke, which is because they have seriously over capitalized their project and cannot fund the holding costs of their projects and nor can they sell, because of the deteriorating market, to recoup their costs.

Think about it, for a declining market can spell disaster for builders and property owners alike, and that especially applies to those who overcapitalize their home and then have to turn around and sell it.

However, for buyers it can signal a wonderful buying opportunity. Suppose the charming salesperson shows you through and pauses to show off the new addition, and with bated breath announces, "of course I should not be telling you this, but the owners tell me their improvements have cost them over half a million dollars." Please do not react to that breach of trust, instead just smile politely and take it on board.

But I have meandered from our home, so that should the gulf be too wide, their property will probably just sit there and remain unsold. Clearly, we should keep looking, and after all the agent has our phone number and we have theirs. So we decide to keep in touch and see what eventuates.

But how does this excessive overpricing happen? It has been a fact of the real estate market in all the years I have been following it. I think in most cases it really comes down to a lack of expertise by the agency guiding the sale, and sometimes it simply boils down to the failure of the owners to take advice, face reality and adjust their price to the marketplace.

I remember the "oil shock" recession of the early 1970s when the price of oil skyrocketed. This happened not long after I had been recruited by the major real estate agency of the day. That recession had stopped the real estate market dead in its tracks. Nothing was happening as the buyers and sellers were poles apart.

This brings us to a very important point, which is that having discovered the real estate we want to buy, it would be very much to our advantage if we understood why the owners are selling. Their motivation is very important to us. Are they just testing the water or do they really need to sell, which we hope is the case? People sell for a variety of reasons: their family may have grown up and left home; there may have been a serious illness; or the breadwinner could have retired and/or sold a business.

If I may return to that recession, this is what I had to do in a hurry. Having been well trained as a salesman by my former American employer, I understood what I had to do. We had a book full of properties for sale; many owners had not seen a salesman for months and felt they had been abandoned while their properties had been on the market seemingly forever. So I set out to interview them individually in order to discover who needed to sell, and to steer them to a position so they could do so.

But to deal with the present, what we are now discovering is that it is not unusual for the agents and their owners to be out of kilter with the market, which makes buying the home of our dreams more difficult than we may have thought. And yet the more property we inspect, and follow through to their sale price, the more we are lifting our skill level and increasing our confidence. Clearly, we need to buy from an owner who needs to sell, and of course eventually we do.

Chapter 2 – Reading the Real Estate Market.

It would be a good idea if we stood back and tried to understand how to read the state of the real estate market. I do not want to be facetious, but asking some agents and/or their sales people about what they think the market is doing is a bit like asking a child how they feel about presents on birthdays and Christmas. We might not be able to read what is precisely happening, but we ought to be able to get near enough to understanding it for our purposes.

On the basis of keeping it simple, let us try to recognize the three more obvious market conditions we may encounter.

They are:

The Booming Market.

The signs of it are everywhere, this market is constantly reported in the media, prices are rising and there are "Sold By" signs all over the place. The auction houses are packed, and stories abound about being outbid. There is a severe shortage of properties for sale, there are low interest rates and banks and lenders generally are lending to all and sundry. Stories circulate of high prices and the couple down the road say they have just refused an enormous offer for their home. The dizzy heights of this market do not last for long, as opportunism and political pressure usually force governments to raise property taxes and/or interest rates. The less perceptive state governments even pass laws in a bid to "manage" it. There are various stages in between which we will leave for the economists.

The Normal Market.

The auction houses are well attended and there is an even flow of property being sold and interest rates are considered settled and moderate. There is a sense of optimism in the air, and the media seem reasonably upbeat about the property and share markets. The lady down the road sells her house after a few weeks, and the new block of apartments near the shopping centre appear to be selling. It is reported that unemployment is steady and that retail sales are healthy.

The Collapsed or Recessionary Market.

The lack of activity in auction rooms and at onsite auctions is hard to miss. There are stories in the media of rising unemployment and you see few advertisements for real estate sales people. The lady down the road still has her house for sale, and it is now covered with real estate signs. The new apartments up near the shopping centre are to be auctioned by the mortgagee in possession. Interest rates are high and there is a general air of doom and gloom. Politicians blame each other while restaurateurs and retailers report that trading is quiet. The cost of borrowing is up, and money is said to be tight, and there is even mention of the dreaded word "recession."

These are of course oversimplifications, and what is actually happening in the market may not be so easily identified. However, at least it has started us thinking about it. If I could make a general observation, in a boom or bust the media can and do get carried away with exaggerated journalism, but if we stick to completing our diligent research it should protect us from making unrealistic decisions.

Chapter 3 – Selling

It is now time to stretch our wings and apply something of what we have learned about the state of the market to the serious business of buying and/or selling. And if we are selling, it is only common sense that access to our property should be made as easy as possible, and so we elect to give the agents a key. Of course they should phone as a matter of courtesy.

If we are selling, our agents need a key.

Now, all our research and diving in and out of properties will have sharpened us, so that we now are aware of what is happening in the marketplace. All of this will help us immeasurably as we go about putting a price on our own property.

Operating in a depressed Market.

Should the market be slow and similar properties to ours are taking a long time to sell, then the price of ours should appear to the agent and buyers alike to be attractive and represent good value. To take that further, I believe that buyers will not make a move unless the price is low enough.

We should discuss this for a moment, the point being that if there are only a few buyers out there, then we are going to have to try harder to attract one. In this sort of market I suggest no signs on the property, as we want our buyer to have the satisfaction of believing they have discovered something special that other buyers may not be aware of. These comments are based on experience, the discipline being to have ours so attractively priced that we knock the opposition out of the running.

Here is an example. An older couple is selling because they can no longer handle the stairs, the garden and general upkeep of the home, and they intend to buy an apartment. They can afford to sell for a low price, because their purchase will also be cheaper than in other conditions. That is, once they have made their sale, they'll be entering a buyers' market which will also offer them a wide range of choice.

But let us not sugar coat what can be a difficult sale to make. Keep an eye on advertising and don't let them overexpose your place, try a few weeks without revealing the address, then let them try an opening, but only occasionally. We understand what is happening in the economy and are determined to move on and do whatever it takes to make our sale.

This can be the right time for an Auction.

During this period, the media and people we talk to are full of doom and gloom. The agents say that nothing much is happening, and comment that buyers expect a bargain. In fact it might be that our agent cannot find a buyer, and eventually he suggests that we hold an auction, and after much discussion we agree.

We have seen their auctioneer in action and we think he puts on a pretty good show. The drama, noise, tension, color and movement, and all the theatre of an auction appeals to us, and we think it is worth a shot, and if it doesn't work, at least we have tried and nothing much is lost. As contradictory as holding an auction in this market may seem, plenty of property has been sold this way when the market seemed as dead as it can be, for it can bring out the bargain hunters, and you only need one to make a sale.

Operating in a steady or normal market.

While we are on the subject of selling, let us consider how we might handle what we see as a normal real estate market. The agents tell us the market is firm, although any price inflation is hardly perceptible. Our own research has told us there is a good supply of property on the market and a wide selection for a buyer to choose from. We agree with the agents that our price should be spot on. Selling might take time, which we must accept, and in order to spread our net we have chosen to give our property to three agents. And having shaved our price down, the agents seemed reasonably content.

But why are we not going to auction? Because in this market our research shows the clearance rate is only fair, and we have to wear the considerable expense, and if it does not sell, we are stuck with no sale and an ongoing sole agency. However, our agents do their job and it is not long before one of them introduces a buyer and we make our sale.

Operating in an overheated or boom market.

Should real estate prices begin to rapidly inflate, we might find ourselves trying to buy or sell in an overheated market, otherwise described as a "boom." Through our research we know prices are rising sharply and are fully aware of what is happening. Our selling price is inflated, and for good reason, and we elect to give it to our chosen agent and to let them handle the mad scramble, which results in three offers in the first week, and we hit our target by the following Tuesday, and by the end of the following day it is all over.

But again, why didn't we auction, especially as the media report that the agents are achieving more than the reserve price? Well, that is because through our research we knew the market was moving, and have adjusted our price accordingly. All we can say is, we have sold ours with no hassles, and importantly, no advertising expenses.

Chapter 4 – Preparing our property

First appearances are very important, and I suggest we cross the road outside our place and look back at our home. What we see is what our buyers will see, so we write a list of all the things we have to do to enhance a buyer's first impression.

Then we call our lawyer and ask them to prepare the necessary documentation, and get them to explain what the legal requirements are that will enable us to make an immediate and binding sale. We instruct them to produce copies to any agent we nominate.

Now, we must methodically put together all the paperwork on the property, and that includes our municipal approval of the extension we did fifteen years ago, and of course collect all the receipts and reports of our pest inspections.

It is generally accepted that it is nigh impossible to form an impartial view of the value of your own property. Nonetheless you should try to keep track of the recent sales of comparable property in your suburb.

We have the minor repairs attended to and clear out the rubbish from the garage and under the house. Clean up the garden and plant some colorful flowers and plants.

When the contract is ready, it is time to call in the agents.

Word of mouth is a good reference. Someone will know of a good agent. Keep asking around until you have three of the best. I suggest the leading advertisers of local real estate would be sensible candidates for the list.

A good real estate salesman is like a hungry tiger and can tie people like you and me up in agreements for sole agencies and auction sales, so fast, we won't even see the pen move. Understanding this, we can now move to carefully establish what our property is worth. From this we will set our very own target, which of course will be our price. We shall keep this handy as we go through the negotiations. Be firm, and have your three chosen agents down individually, and ask them to put in writing what they think the property is worth, and what they think the market is doing.

Do not get sidetracked into longwinded discussions about the benefits or otherwise of auctions, sole agencies, chain franchise listings, or anything else. All we want to know is their opinion of value, and what they think the market is doing. Do not feel guilty about launching into this brain picking exercise, because the agents are used to it, and expect it. Rest assured that they will soon be back with their letters.

So we understand what is going to happen, we will pause a moment to look at all this through the agents' eyes. They live in fear of losing out to a rival agent who has quoted a higher price.

I might dwell on why and how this happens. The over-quoting of an expected sale price for your home is an irresponsible act, and certainly in Australia is a complete breach of the agent's duty to their vendor. Unfortunately, it can also be ridiculously wide of the mark. The cause can be an inexperienced salesperson or agent, whom we should do our best to avoid altogether.

There are also sharp and manipulative agents who are intent on tying you up while they go through the motions of trying to sell you property. The benefits to them are that in the marketplace, they are seen to have a new property for sale, which is kudos in itself. They have access to those buyers who inspect it, and whom they can switch to another home. They also have the opportunity to meet any future vendors who are out and about to investigate the market. Meanwhile, we wonder why our home has not been sold.

Experienced agents are keen judges of what a home is worth. But their problem is that they do not know how we will react when they tell us. So they avoid the issue, and see the way out as being a period of attrition during which they will attempt to have us steadily adjust the price down to a level at which they can sell.

All we want is a trouble-free sale, but for them it is a matter of having to earn an income, which is why they prefer to tie you up into an exclusive arrangement, that is, to become the sole agent for an auction sale, which usually runs for three or four weeks prior to the auction date, and anything up to two or three months after.

The way the system has evolved in Australia, the vendor is expected to pay for the advertising and fees of a sale by auction, which can be considerable.

May we return to those all-important letters? We have received three opinions of value, and there is little variation between them. Their opinions of the state of the market are also fairly similar. We have come a long way, and together with our own research, we have formed a considered opinion of what our property is worth.

This presents us with a variety of options:

1. We can create a sole agency for an auction or a sale by private treaty for a favored agent.

2. We can give them all an ordinary agency for a sale by private treaty.

3. Or we might join two of them in a joint agency for a private treaty sale or a sale by auction.

Despite all the effort and money spent by agents on promoting their system, the reality is that how you sell will have little bearing on the price you achieve. Of course what is missing in all this is the all important ingredient of trust. Hence, agents will launch into a long winded rigmarole about auctions, the tremendous benefits of their exclusive marketing plan, and so on. Most of this is rubbish, as how we sell is simply a matter of preference.

But let us return to the difficulty of putting a price on our home. It is perfectly understandable that subconsciously or otherwise, we will be biased, as we have lived there and this is the place of our memories. We know the neighbors, planted and established the garden, and drove our own and their children to school. Selling our home is going to be a large emotional wrench.

Chapter 5 – Investigating Our Real Estate

Buyers, it is time to thoroughly investigate our chosen piece of real estate.

Having realized that our research is starting to pay big dividends, it probably will not be long before we discover the property we want to buy.

And so it is time for us to consider that possibility, for wherever you buy, the laws of disclosure and misrepresentation by the owner may vary, and we do not want to be involved in a legal battle. Our aim is to discover the precise physical condition and legal status of the property before we commit ourselves.

There are shoddy builders, and owners who paper and patch over serious faults, there is concrete cancer, structural rust, wood rot, borers and termites. There are homes built where it floods and others where the sewer has never been connected. There are homes where the boundary fences are not in the right place and where the driveway encroaches upon a neighbor. There are also homes and multi-storey apartment buildings with rising damp, structural cracks and missing expansion joints. Doubly check the zoning: is there a new supermarket about to be built down the road that will completely change the character of the neighborhood?

Fortunately, most of us will never be confronted with these disasters, but they do happen, and so before we leave this topic, we should also consider the state of the building's current management.

Beware of apartment buildings where the owners are in a perpetual state of unresolved legal and domestic argument.

I only mention these to highlight the importance of completing our diligent searches before we enter into a binding contract.

When our legal adviser says that our copy of the contract appears to be in order, we should ask if in our state there is a legal device that we and an owner can enter into that will bind the transaction while we you complete the necessary inspections and searches. It is now time to employ a building inspector, a surveyor and a pest inspector, and in my view, even an architect and engineer to resolve any doubts you may have about the property. Make it a rule never to commit without first getting thorough written reports on the physical state of the property. Should it be an apartment, ensure your report says the building's books have been inspected and are in order, and beware of those buildings with serious structural faults, unresolved legal problems, or high maintenance and running costs.

Chapter 6 – The Negotiation.

This is where you will reap the reward of carefully doing your research, as you will have confidence in your own opinion and know where you stand. The negotiation is not difficult to undertake, and in our educated and sophisticated society most of us can handle the sale or purchase of the family car, a washing machine and a boat. The main difference is that in real estate the price is fluid, and in most cases negotiable, and of course the stakes are very much higher.

There are a few ground rules to follow when buying or selling. Most people will only be involved in one or two transactions during our lives. Therefore, we should understand that it is during the negotiation when the skill of the agent or salesperson will come into play. We should have a target price; see Chapter 4.

The reality of a real estate transaction is that no one can force a vendor to accept an offer, just as no one can force a buyer to make one. These are considered and logical decisions the parties agree to make and stick by, while the enquiries and legal requirements are completed.

The watchwords here should be "reasonableness" and "flexibility," which should assist buyer and seller to move from their positions on the price so that their deal can be struck. But to return to those ground rules:

If you are selling and an offer is made on your property and it is unacceptable, tell the agent straight away to refuse it. Do not leave a buyer dangling as the more time they have to think about their position the more entrenched in it they become.

Chapter 7 – Readying to enter the Market

We have decided what figure we are prepared to pay as a buyer, and the price we want to achieve as a seller. The position of both parties will be clear if we consider the offers made during this transaction. We place our property on the market with an asking price of $1.800, 000. The reality is we would be happy to achieve around $1,700,000 which becomes our "target," to be kept in the forefront of our mind.

Try to simplify the negotiation by restricting the number of offers. From our side we should aim to make significant and considered adjustments to our price.

This is how we should go about it:

Our agent reports that our buyers are a couple who are very attracted to our property, they particularly appreciate the landscaping, and the style of the home itself, and can picture themselves living in it.

Our buyers open the negotiation with an offer of $1,600, 000.

Wearing our vendor's hat, this is the first offer we have received, and as our property has been on the market for seven weeks, we are keen to negotiate. We respond to our buyer's first offer of $1,600,000 by making a counter offer to sell at $1,700,000.

The sequence of offers runs like this:

1. Buyer $1,600,000   first offer.
2. Vendor $1,700,000 first counter offer.
3. Buyer $1,650,000 second offer.
4. Vendor $1,675,000 second counter offer

Remember our target was set at $1,700,000.

This is an excellent sign that both parties want this negotiation to succeed. That evening a negotiated price of $1,665,000 is agreed upon. The exchange of contracts, including the payment of the deposit takes place not long after. In Australia the deposit is usually 10% but is variable and in a tough market the vendor might agree to accept 5%.

A few tips for both parties should assist the negotiations:

Keep the conversations with the agent short, and do not react to their shock, horror, or other comments. They are skilled at moving buyers and sellers from their assumed positions as they maneuver them toward the desired result. If you are selling and you refuse an offer, do show your intent, and give the agent a counter offer that moves you closer to your target. The agent knows only too well what the property is likely to sell for, and they are going to push for a result. They will not get paid unless they can achieve one. As the negotiation nears its completion, do remember our watchwords so that neither party becomes entrenched in their position. If the last offer is close, grab the deal with both hands and get on with your life.

Chapter 8 – Buying and Selling Investment Property

This market is about money and nothing else. The fact that land and bricks and mortar are being traded has little to do with it, and as such it is tough and unforgiving. The attitude is that the deal either stacks up or it does not.

I assume you have read the previous chapters, and understand the importance of comparing like with like, and of diligently doing your research. The difference here is that this market is mainly concerned with a property's *yield*, because it is the yield that determines value, and to arrive at that we need the precise figures of the income and outgoings(taxes and upkeep) of any property we are looking at.

Net return refers to the property's annual income after deducting all annual outgoings, and the yield refers to that return expressed as a percent of the sale price of the property. For example:

Sale price	$1,000,000

Annual income	+$100,000
Less annual Outgoings	-$40,000
Net income	**$60,000**

The *yield* is determined as net income divided by the price. Therefore-

$$\frac{\$60{,}000 \text{ net income}}{\$1{,}000{,}000 \text{ sale price}} = 6.00\%$$

Therefore, if we paid $950,000 the yield would be 6.3%.

And if we paid $900,000 it would be 6.6%.

At $800,000 it would be 7.5%.

At $700,000 it would be 8.5% and so on.

So *the lower the price, the higher the yield.*

If we are contemplating the sale or purchase of investment property, a yield table such as this will help to clarify our thoughts. And to take it further, we now know that this property sold for $800.000 with a yield of 7.5%. Therefore, we now know that a similar property in a similar location should also sell for a yield of close to 7.5%.

Tenanted property such as shopping centers, office blocks, factories and blocks of apartments will be said to have sold showing a yield of such and such.

For instance we realize that if modern shops in a good neighborhood sell at a yield of six per cent, and we can buy a group of similar shops with a yield of six point nine per cent, we are definitely heading down the right track.

Let us look at the effect of the difference of those yields will have on the purchase price.

Our investment report shows that the annual income of these shops is-- $400,000.

The annual outgoings are $90,000.

Therefore the net income is $310,000.

Reversing the process to get a desired yield of 6%, we take $310,00 divided by 0.06 gives us a value of $5,166,666.

Now watch the relationship between price and yield:

At 6.0% the price is $5,166,666.
At 6.9% the price is $4,492,753.

The difference of a 0.9 % gives us a theoretical savings of $673,913, which is of course significant.

Leaving that example behind us, the three vital pieces of information we need to obtain are the net income, the price, and the yield, but if you only have *two* of them, you can work out the third.

Arm yourself with a pocket calculator and you are in business, as:

- Income divided by Price = Yield

- Income divided by Yield = Price.

- Price x Yield = Income.

However, we cannot take a supplied set of figures at face value. They need to be checked for accuracy and completeness, in particular that no item of cost has been overlooked. Items like insurance need to be gone into thoroughly: are all compulsory policies costed in, is there enough cover and is the building covered on a new for old basis? Start again, get new quotes for the whole lot and compare your against their figures?

At the start of this chapter, I played down the importance of the land and the bricks and mortar standing upon it. I confess that I did this so we would focus on the importance of doing research. The funds needed to have a stake in this market can be very large indeed, so of course the improvements on the land are very important.

This is a time to cultivate an experienced property lawyer who is familiar with commercial leases and contracts, and understands the pitfalls of dealing in this market. We should also cultivate a relationship with a builder, an architect and a civil engineer. As a general rule I would steer clear of small suburban shop and office buildings with flat roofs, as they are a cheap finish and can be an ongoing nightmare. What was the previous use of the land? For example, is it landfill, and if it is what can we find out about it? Modern multi rise buildings need to be designed and built so that their roofs drain and prevent pooling.

We need to know if the lifts are modern and have been well maintained. Similarly, we need to check that the air conditioning plant functions as it should, is modern and it is very important that is has been fastidiously maintained.

Those who trade in this market tend to specialize and develop an expertise in buying and selling in a particular segment, and might specialize in retail space, hotels, blocks of apartments, factories, office buildings and so on. They develop an ability to see different avenues for their investment, look at issues like potential future subdivision, its worth to an owner occupier, the effects of a quick makeover on cash flow. If the letting market is flat, is it worth more to an owner occupier, or can it be subdivided and given separate titles and resold at a handy profit?

As I said at the start, when it comes to investment property, it is all about money, it is about investing it wisely, and hopefully accumulating a great pile of it, and I hope this book will help you do just that.

Appendix: On Borrowing

A few notes on borrowing funds to buy your home.

Few of us are in that most enviable of situations where we can pay cash for our home. Which brings us to the point of considering the source of funds, since that institution shall hold the first mortgage over our home. Think about it, because if we should get into financial difficulty through sickness, being retrenched, a business downturn or similar, it is to them that we have to go cap in hand as we ask for their help in rearranging our mortgage repayments. This single fact may give them immense power over our lives.

Certainly in Sydney, we are at our most vulnerable during the first four or so years of the mortgage. After that, the value of our home should have inflated to give us significantly more equity and therefore more control over our borrowing. There is no rule that says that this must happen, but in most of the major cities in Australia it just does.

Buyers have a choice of borrowing from banks, building societies, insurance companies, credit unions, and other institutions. My view is that Australian building societies offer a most attractive avenue for home finance and I strongly recommend them.

About the Author

Sydney is one of the great cities of the world and settlement has radiated out from the shores of the beautiful harbor which was first settled in 1788. It has never stopped growing from that humble beginning. My career began in 1966 as a real estate salesman on the North Shore which now in 2013 has a towering skyline of office and apartment buildings. This has been an exciting time to have played a small roll in this dynamic growth, which has enabled me to sell everything from office buildings, factories, rows of shops, shopping centre sites, apartment buildings, magnificent harbor side homes and penthouses.

I qualified as a valuer and became the manager at Neutral Bay for the premier real estate agency of that time. It has been a privilege to have been a part of it, for through it I have met a host of wonderful people including, giants of industry, eminent Judges and legal luminaries, as well as Hollywood stars, State Premiers and Prime Ministers. But it is to the many ordinary people from all walks of life who gave me their trust, and went on to borrow what must have seemed like an obscene amount of money so they might establish a home. To them I would like to offer my sincere and heartfelt thank you.

Geoffrey Hope Gibson